SEEKERS OF TRUTH

— Finding the Faith —

by Rosalie McPhee

MADONNA HOUSE PUBLICATIONS
Combermere, Ontario, Canada

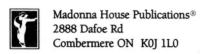

Madonna House Publications®
2888 Dafoe Rd
Combermere ON K0J 1L0

www.madonnahouse.org/publications

© 2002 Madonna House Publications. All rights reserved.

No part of this work may be reproduced, stored in a retrieval system or trans-mitted in any form or by any means, electronic, mechanical, or otherwise, without express written permission. The Our Lady of Combermere colophon is a registered trade-mark of Madonna House Publications.

First Edition

First printing, July 3, 2002 — feast of St. Thomas

Printed in Canada

Scripture texts in this work are taken from the *New American Bible with Revised New Testament and Psalms* © 1991, 1986, 1970 Confraternity of Christian Doctrine, Washington, D.C. All Rights Reserved.

Quotations from Pope John Paul II are taken from: Letter to the Youth of the World, Homily 5/8/90, Homily 6/15/84, Young People to Assisi 8/18/01, and World Youth Day 1991, 1992, 1993, 1997, 1999 and 2002.

National Library of Canada Cataloguing in Publication Data

McPhee, Rosalie, 1948–
  Seekers of truth: finding the faith

ISBN 0-921440-81-2

  1. McPhee, Rosalie, 1948–. 2. Catholic converts—Canada—Biography.
3. Spiritual biography—Canada. I. Title.

BL73.M32A3 2002   282'.092   C2002-902813-2

Design and cover photo by Rob Huston

This book is set in Berkeley, designed by Frederic W. Goudy for the University of California Press in 1938. Heading and quotation text is set in Christiana, designed by Gudrun Zapf von Hesse for the Berthold foundry in 1991.

CONTENTS

Introduction 5

Are You There, God? 9

The Restless Search 12

What is Freedom? 15

All we need is Love 18

Non-Conformity 21

Learning our Vocation 25

Encountering God 29

The Living Bread 33

What Do You Believe? 36

Obstacles to Grace 38

Blessed Poverty 40

Shine Your Light 43

God's Incredible Mercy 47

Our Mother Mary 49

Coming Home 53

Taking the Leap 58

My Lord God, I have no idea where I am going. I do not see the road ahead of me. I cannot know for certain where it will end. Nor do I really know myself, and the fact that I think that I am following your will does not mean that I am actually doing so. But I believe that the desire to please you does in fact please you. And I hope I have that desire in all that I am doing. I hope that I will never do anything apart from that desire. And I know that if I do this you will lead me by the right road though I may know nothing about it. Therefore will I trust you always though I may seem to be lost and in the shadow of death. I will not fear, for you are ever with me, and you will never leave me to face my perils alone.

— Thomas Merton
Thoughts in Solitude

INTRODUCTION

Allow your hearts to be intoxicated with
the life which Jesus offers you; in him your
true youthfulness lies.

— Pope John Paul II

As I look back on the arduous and criss-crossing journey we undertook as we
searched for God, I wonder at how many
wrong turns we took. How many times we
danced blindfolded on the precipice, unafraid
because our spiritual eyes could not see. How
tenderly God cared for us, pulling us back
each time we teetered on the edge.

As we dabbled in so many occult and
New Age practises, we learned firsthand how
fallen angels masquerade as apparently harmless angels of light. The word 'occult' is
formed from the Latin word 'occultare',
meaning 'to hide from sight', and this is the
way the evil one works. God allowed us to
recognize and avoid the darkness, even
before we moved into the light.

After coming into the Church, we were taught the importance of renouncing all connections with the occult world, in order to be truly free of its veiled but enduring influence. But God is so much bigger than all of that, and doesn't want us to live in fear. Jesus has already won the victory!

We cannot live in two worlds and live in the fullness that God intended for us. He wants all of us. He tells us: "Whoever is not with me is against me" (Lk 11:23) Once we use our own wills to turn away from darkness, we are freed from the shackles that bind us. We are able to fully embrace God, our Creator, our Daddy— and to allow ourselves to be led by the Holy Spirit.

We had the right idea in seeking Love and Peace and Joy. If only we had realized earlier that they all come from God himself, and he will give them to us if we draw close to him. They are attainable, on one condition—that we learn to embrace the Cross.

We each have tailor-made crosses, and only God knows his purpose in designing them for us. If we can learn to go beyond accepting them to truly *embracing* them, then we will grow into that person God created us to be. Each time we say 'yes' to God, each time we raise our hearts to him in total submission, we draw a little closer to the source of true joy.

> We know that all things work for good for those who love God, who are called according to his purpose.
>
> — Rom 8:28

Not everyone needs to take the winding road to God that we did. However, it will be a narrow road, and it may be lonely at times. But he will always walk beside us, and pick us up tenderly and carry us when we stumble. And our mother Mary will be right beside him, lovingly accompanying and protecting us along the way.

> The Church needs your energies, your enthusiasm, your youthful ideals, in order to make the Gospel of Life penetrate the fabric of society, transforming people's hearts and the structures

of society in order to create a civilization of
true justice and love.

— Pope John Paul II

ARE YOU THERE, GOD?

When I see your heavens, the work of your
fingers, the moon and stars that you set in
place—What are humans that you are
mindful of them, mere mortals that you
care for them? Yet you have made them little less than a god, crowned them with
glory and honor.

— Ps 8:4-6

It was one of those nights when you see so
many more stars than usual, and I pondered as I gazed at the vastness of the clear
starry sky. How far away were the stars? It
was staggering to try and think of light years,
but whatever the distance was, what was
beyond that? And then beyond that—where
is the edge of space? If there were an edge
then there would be something on the other
side of the edge, and what would be beyond
that? Suddenly I knew there was a God! This
concept of going on forever, without any

boundary or end, was like God. I knew unquestionably now that he existed.

> Our restless hearts seek beyond our limits, challenging our capacity to think and love; to think and love the immeasurable, the infinite, the absolute and supreme form of Being. Our inner eye looks upon the unlimited horizons of our hopes and aspirations. And in the midst of all life's contradictions, we seek the true meaning of life. We wonder and we ask ourselves "why?" Why am I here? Why do I exist? What must I do?
>
> — Pope John Paul II

My heart leapt, because I KNEW—that which I had been wondering and questioning and doubting for a number of years! It wasn't an argument or debate that had been won, it was just a sudden quiet knowing—and realizing that this KNOWING was a gift from God, who made me and everything else! All the lights went on in my darkened mind, and it was God's light! I wanted to know so much more about him, but I realized that people had many different ideas about him. I didn't want ideas, or speculation, or opinion; I only wanted the TRUTH!

God alone is the infinite horizon of your life.

— Pope John Paul II

THE RESTLESS SEARCH

You have made us for yourself, O Lord,
and our hearts are restless until they rest
in you.

— St. Augustine

When I met my husband, Don, we were
both seeking the same thing, and as
we joined our lives, we joined together in our
pursuit of Truth. We read books about
Hinduism and Buddhism, both ancient texts
and North American popular offshoots. We
had friends who were Scientologists, some
who were Sufis, some who practised
Transcendental Meditation, and even some
who professed to receive 'messages' from
'Space Brothers' through meditation. I studied
astrology, and learned the mathematical way
to cast a horoscope. We read books on
Theosophy. None of these things seemed to
be right for us; so, like most people of the
sixties generation, we picked and chose those
things which appealed to us, and formed our

own personal system of beliefs. But I knew they were our *own*, and were only a stopgap until we found the whole real truth. The last place we looked was the Catholic Church, and then we stumbled inadvertently into it.

> In a culture which holds that no universally valid truths are possible, nothing is absolute. Therefore, in the end they say—objective goodness and evil no longer really matter. Good comes to mean what is pleasing or useful at a particular moment. Evil means what contradicts our subjective wishes. Each person can build a private system of values.
>
> — Pope John Paul II

Our search for the truth created a constant restlessness in us, causing us to travel from place to place in our quest. We painted a small bus with flowers and hearts, and furnished it inside to make a compact but comfortable home. It was a secure and loving place, and we discarded all our possessions except what would fit into the bus. Travelling across the country and back, all we found were other people searching, and some who had adopted strange beliefs. None satisfied us; some downright scared us.

Today youth has itchy soles. They criss-cross the world like a lost tribe seeking a place where somebody will really tell them without words that they love them... They seek God, in so many words, and God will be given to them by you and me if we have faith and are filled with hope and love.

— Catherine Doherty

WHAT IS FREEDOM?

If you remain in my word, you will truly be
my disciples, and you will know the truth,
and the truth will set you free.

— Jn 8:31-32

It was a dangerous precipice we walked
along, with no clear discernment of good
and evil, and no solid moral value system.
Even though we lived and travelled among
people of similar persuasions, each one was a
little different because each person formed
their own code (which could change with the
wind), and so it was hard to trust one another completely.

It is good to pause and look back, and to see
the mercy and grace of God leading us
through so many dangerous paths and quick-
sand to the place where we are today. Let this
backward glance give us courage for today and
readiness for tomorrow.

— Catherine Doherty

We had strong ideals, and rejected materialism and the 'system' that supported and created it. World peace and universal brotherhood were our goals, as well as a simple lifestyle, which eventually led us to settle in rural areas. We became experts on going against the grain and accepted persecution in return. Many times we were insulted, kicked out of restaurants, or called 'freaks' because of the length of our hair or the way we dressed. Stubbornly, we adopted the term 'freaks' for ourselves, rather than use the media's favourite name—'hippies'.

> To be truly free does not at all mean doing everything that pleases me, or doing what I want to do. Freedom contains in itself the criterion of truth, the discipline of truth. To be truly free means to use one's own freedom for what is a true good. Continuing therefore: to be truly free means to be a person of upright conscience, to be responsible, to be a person 'for others'.
>
> — Pope John Paul II

In our search for freedom, we rejected many good solid principles. Our need for a clearly defined value system was so great, although we didn't realize it at the time. Like children, we inwardly craved discipline and order in our lives, while outwardly rejecting both.

♭ What we desire most of all is freedom. The world today would like to be free of all of this mess that we are in, but the price of freedom is what nobody wants to pay. The price of freedom is submission, obedience: he who is obedient is free.

— Catherine Doherty

ALL WE NEED IS LOVE

> This is my commandment, that you love
> one another as I have loved you. Greater
> love has no man than this, that a man lay
> down his life for his friends. You are my
> friends if you do what I command you.
>
> — Jn 15:12-14

He called himself Johnny Wren. We travelled the grass-roots folk music circuit
on the west coast, and played at small con-
certs and craft fairs together. We wrote and
sang about peace and freedom and love, and
how we were all going to change the world.
Johnny had a solo act, and had a following of
young women who loved to brush his hip-
length shiny black hair. He seemed to have
adopted the identity of a little waif, and at 22
years old had the regular habit of sucking his
thumb, in or out of the public eye. It rather
irritated me, because I felt it was an act, and
that he lacked sincerity and truth.

One day when Don and I were walking down the street with him, we started to argue about the sincerity of our lives and the sincerity of our music and message—basically who was the most loving and the most peaceful and the most honest. Our conversation, mostly between Johnny and me, was getting more and more heated, and drawing the attention of passers-by.

Finally, in frustration, and in trying to prove my point, I said:

"I mean what's this nonsense about sucking your thumb, anyway? You're just trying to project an image of yourself as this lovable little boy!!"

I quickly realized that I had pushed a button, and he started to shout hysterically, over and over again: "So what if I suck my thumb?! So what if I suck my thumb?! So what if I suck my thumb?!...on an on.

Acting on impulse, I slapped him in the face. Immediately, he slapped me back. Before I knew it, Don's knee-jerk defence of me was to give him a bloody nose. We stood in shock and looked at one another, suddenly realizing the import of what had happened. We stared at each other in disbelief, and then started to laugh and laugh at ourselves. How hollow our "message" of peace and love was. We hugged and begged forgiveness of one another, each of us in tears. By this time we had attracted quite a crowd of onlookers, who clapped and cheered at this street drama!

Whatever you did for one of these least brothers of mine, you did for me.

— Mt 25:40

Non-Conformity

Do not conform yourselves to this age but be transformed by the renewal of your mind, that you may discern what is the will of God, what is good and pleasing and perfect.

— Rom 12:2

We arrived at the Earthwood Farm as the sun was setting. This was to be our new home, and the fulfillment of a dream. We were elated to have been invited to help form a new back-to-the-land community that would be dedicated to organic farming and development of alternative power sources, in the beautiful hills of Kentucky. It wasn't your regular hippie community though: it was funded by a millionaire who was the father of one of the founders. It was to have the best of everything: the best organic and vegetarian food, the best goats, hens that laid blue eggs, new oak barns, solar homes—anything this millionaire's daughter and her partner could dream up.

God really does have a sense of humour, and must have been chuckling to himself as he set this one up for us. So you have a dream, and you think it's the ultimate and will make you happy—well here it is—try it on for a while, and see if it does the trick!

Well, it did—but not in the way we thought. He got us where he wanted us by using what we *thought* we wanted, and instead offered us what we *really* wanted. And he placed the two side-by-side for an obvious comparison.

They say if you eat steak every day, or ice cream—you get sick of them. That's how we began to feel about having the best of everything we had ever dreamed. We began to feel an emptiness, a restlessness, and a feeling of "is this all there is?"

Dear young people, do not be content with anything less than the highest ideals! Do not let yourselves be dispirited by those who are disillusioned with life and have grown deaf to the deepest and most authentic desires of their heart. You are right to be disappointed with hollow entertainment and passing fads, and with aiming at too little in life. If you have an ardent desire for the Lord you will steer clear of the mediocrity and conformism so widespread in our society.

— Pope John Paul II

In our dogged effort to be non-conformists, we had been really been conforming to a tide of rebellion. Many of the principles we had adopted and adapted went against the truth that Jesus taught. How strange to realize that we could be more radical by conforming our lives to Jesus' clear gospel teachings!

When it comes to any compromise with the message of the gospel, there can be no giving ground. Christ said very clearly, he who is not with me is against me. The Christian and the whole Church must cry out loudly and uncompromisingly the glad news, even if the world considers it bad news, disturbing news, unpleasant news. Christ came to disturb the consciences of men. The people who continue his mission must also continue to disturb.

— Catherine Doherty

LEARNING OUR VOCATION

For you see, marriage is a vocation, a call
of God to two people to become one,
found a home, beget, bear, and raise children; and, in this glorious and very hard
vocation, to become saints themselves, and
to do all that is in their power to make
saints of their children.

— Catherine Doherty

When we heard of a neighbouring community with young families much like
us, we jumped at the chance to go and visit.
They were called the Families of St. Benedict.
We'd heard they were Catholics and rather
religious, but we considered ourselves open-
minded—and anyway—we were desperate
for something more than what we had. We
dropped in for a visit one day, and were surprised to see how much we had in common
with them. They even dressed much like us,
and as they told their stories, we realized that
they had come from backgrounds very similar

to our own, but had found or rediscovered God in the Catholic Church. This was fascinating to us. We hadn't dreamed that people like them, people like us, could be drawn to the Catholic Church.

We got along so well that we went back again, and were always welcomed warmly. The Families of St. Benedict lived beside The Abbey of Gethsemane, a Trappist monastery. There they attended daily mass and received spiritual direction. Although they were not monks, they told us that their vocation was to marriage and family. Their life was a type of monastic family life, in voluntary poverty. Their homes were simple and handmade, without any electricity. They prayed together three times a day, and had two hours of "quiet time" in the afternoon, when the children would rest.

They told us more about the monastery, and we were fascinated to hear of the lives of these celibate monks. As I saw how busy our children kept us, and those of this community, I could see how the celibate vocation freed the monks to dedicate their lives to pray for us all. We learned that even though the monastery was cloistered, the chapel had a balcony that was open to the public for mass or to hear the monks chanting their prayers seven times a day.

To set out on the path of the married vocation means to learn married love day by day, year by year: love according to soul and body, love that "is patient, is kind, that does not insist on its own way...and does not rejoice at wrong": love that "rejoices in the right:, love that "endures all things".

– Pope John Paul II

One of the things that really struck us about the Families of St. Benedict was how they cherished their children. At Earthwood Farm, our two were the only children as of yet, and sometimes we felt they were treated as more of an inconvenience than the gift we knew them to be. When we visited the Families of St Benedict our children were treated with such warmth and love, and all the children played so happily together. Our instinctive knowledge that life is a gift was confirmed by the love we saw in their families.

♭ God created man in his image; in the divine image he created him; male and female he created them. God blessed them, saying: "Be fertile and multiply.

— Gen 1:27-28

Encountering God

Prayer must lead us to total surrender, or it will lead us nowhere except back to ourselves. It is this surrender that we fear so much, and this is why prayer is such a fearsome and dangerous thing...Do not fool yourself: Once you encounter God, you will no longer be the same person you were before.

— Catherine Doherty

Tall gum trees flanked the long driveway as we drove up to the monastery. We passed through a small graveyard on our way to the chapel entrance, and I was comforted and reassured by a little stone angel that seemed to be welcoming us. There wasn't much nightlife in rural Kentucky, and we were going to hear the monks chant Compline. It was very much like going to a concert for us—to be entertained. But we didn't know what God had in store for us.

We were a little nervous, afraid that we might be refused entrance.

> Dear young people, like the first disciples, follow Jesus! Do not be afraid to draw near to Him, to cross the threshold of his dwelling, to speak with Him, face to face, as you talk with a friend. (cf. Ex 33:11)
>
> — Pope John Paul II

We walked up the stone stairs that led to the balcony, and as we entered I was struck by something—what was it? It was powerful. I looked up at the tall stone walls, and listened to the echo of the monks shuffling in to take their places facing one another on either side of the chapel. They were in their traditional white hooded robes, their hands folded in their sleeves as they reverently entered. What was this I was feeling? It wasn't really fear, but it was very strong whatever it was. It certainly didn't feel like a concert hall. A few other people were quietly filing into the balcony.

When they started to chant, I became absolutely transfixed. It was beautiful, captivating, and I was completely taken over by the music. It was so much more than just music. It sounded like…angels…a heavenly choir! Something came over me, and realized that what I had felt when I came in was *the presence of God*. And these men were praying to this God, their God, *my* God. Their chanting was truly reaching up to God and touching him, as it was touching me. I *knew* that He was real, and that their faith was real, and God was reaching out to me through them. I was filled with awe, and felt that a hunger in me was beginning to be filled.

Wanting to recreate this experience, we learned to chant these Compline Psalms together in the evening, and this became our daily prayer.

For me, prayer means launching out of the heart toward God; it means lifting up one's eyes, quite simply, to heaven, a cry of grateful love from the crest of joy or the trough of despair; it's a vast, supernatural force which opens out my heart, and binds me close to Jesus.

— St. Thérèse of Lisieux

THE LIVING BREAD

I am the living bread that came down from heaven; whoever eats this bread will live forever; and the bread that I will give is my flesh for the life of the world.

— Jn 6:51

We began to attend masses at the monastery. With no experience of the Catholic Church, we just followed what other people were doing—stood when they stood, kneeled when they kneeled—and went and received communion when they did. We had no idea that what we were doing was not acceptable—we tried to do the right thing, and assumed that following what others were doing *was* the right way.

After a couple of weeks of this, one of the monks came up to us after mass and spoke to us. He was friendly and kind, but he told us that we could not receive communion any-more, although we could come to mass and prayers whenever we wished. He explained that as Catholics they believed that the piece of bread, which still looked like bread, *really* became Jesus at the mass.

> It is there in the mystery of the Eucharist that we get the strength to live the law of love. Why? Because, you can barely step onto the threshold of this mystery, the tips of your toes scarcely reach. This mystery is so blinding, so incredible, that few can enter into it further. He is the Bridegroom, and we are all His Beloved. All men and women are His Brides. He wants to introduce all of us to His Father. It is through the Bread and Wine that God and I become one.
>
> — Catherine Doherty

At the next mass we attended, when it came to Communion time, we obediently stayed kneeling while everyone else went up to receive Communion. As I knelt there, I was filled with a longing, and I started to cry—soft quiet tears. A tremendous grace overcame me, and I suddenly *knew* that what the monk had told us was true—*it really was Jesus that they were receiving!* Glancing over at

Don, I knew before he said anything, that he had the same experience. We *knew*—and never doubted from then on—and the hunger for Jesus in the Eucharist would continue to draw us into the Catholic Church.

Call out to Jesus to remain with you always along the many roads to Emmaus of our time. May He be your strength, your point of reference, your enduring hope. May the Eucharistic Bread, dear young people, never be lacking on the tables of your existence. And may you draw from this Bread the strength to bear witness to the faith!

— Pope John Paul II

What Do You Believe?

"Young people, do not be afraid to be holy!" Fly high, be among those whose goals are worthy of sons and daughters of God. Glorify God in your lives!

— Pope John Paul II

The Families of St. Benedict suggested we might like to visit with one of the monks who had been designated as a liaison between the monastery and their community. He would be allowed to talk to us, unlike most of the monks whose vow of silence prevented them. This was the opportunity we had been seeking for so long. The idea scared us a little—these holy monks in their long robes seemed more angelic than human to us. Would he really accept and understand us? But we had so many questions to ask. So we plucked up our courage and made an appointment with him.

When we saw Brother Frederic waiting outside for us in his patched denim jeans and his ball cap, we were amazed at the transformation. With a smile on his face, he looked so approachable, so human, that we were able to launch right into all our questions without reserve. What do you believe? Who is God? What is life about? Why are we here? What does it mean to be holy?

Holiness is not one exercise or another, it consists in a disposition of the heart, which renders us humble and little in the hands of God, conscious of our weakness but confident, even daringly confident, in his fatherly goodness.

— St. Thérèse of Lisieux

He answered each of our questions simply and directly and we began to hear a song echoing in our hearts, a deep and powerful "Yes!" as we listened. We knew without doubt that he spoke the truth we had been waiting for. We were called to holiness, too. A fire began to burn in us that nothing could extinguish!

OBSTACLES TO GRACE

> Be perfect, just as your heavenly Father is
> perfect.
>
> — Mt 5:48

We would go for long walks among the fields and woods of the beautiful monastery farm. He answered our questions and fed our hunger by leading us through the Apostles' Creed, one line at a time. He explained exalted truths in down-to-earth language, without removing the mystery. We couldn't get enough.

One day, as we were walking with him through peaceful woods, with wildflowers strewn along the path, I felt a joy and euphoria that almost made me want to skip. Walking a little ahead of him and Don, I suddenly stopped in my tracks. There in the middle of this isolated forest, with no signs of human presence anywhere in sight, was a bronze figure, life-sized. I walked up to it, and stared at it in amazement. He was kneeling, with his hands outstretched upwards, and his face etched in grief and pain. It looked like Jesus, and as Brother Frederic and Don caught up with me, it was confirmed.

"What is it? Why is he in such pain?" I asked naively.

Brother Frederic looked at me and smiled. "He's preparing himself for his terrible suffering and death—for all of us. He pointed over to another statue through the trees a bit, which I hadn't noticed. I walked over and saw the three disciples, leaning on one another, all blissfully fast asleep. "Just when he needed his friends most to stay with him," continued Brother Frederic, "they fell asleep. Just like us…"

> Sin cuts us off sharply from God's friendship. Losing God, we stand alone. How insignificant, how small we are without Him! Let us meditate on this, and ask the Lord for tears of repentance to wash the stain of all sin from our souls.
>
> — Catherine Doherty

BLESSED POVERTY

Gradually, without knowing it, we have come to trust more in money than in God. From earliest childhood, modern man is brought up to value money above all else, and even to value himself by his capacity for getting it.

— Catherine Doherty

We felt suspended between two worlds. Our 'dream' community had almost unlimited physical wealth, but terrible spiritual poverty. The Families of St. Benedict, which drew us like a moth to a flame, had a vow of physical poverty, but unlimited spiritual wealth, drawn from the Catholic Church. We knew that we could drink and drink from its waters of life, and they would never be used up.

Blessed are you who are poor, for the kingdom of God is yours.

— Lk 6:20

In discussing this with Brother Frederic, he said he thought he might know a house we could move into. He called us back the next day, to say he had a place for us: it was a five-minute walk to the monastery chapel, and the rent was free! These neighbours were friends of the monastery, and had built a new home closer to the road Their old home was unoccupied, and they generously offered to let us live there.

It turned out that it had been unoccupied for a number of years. We walked up the steps of the porch, fell through a hole in the floor, and noticed a dead opossum underneath. The running water wasn't running too well, but one bonus was that the house was filled with antiques that the owners were storing there. They told us that we were welcome to use them. It wasn't a great house, but it would be great for us. We had lived in places before which were no better—we'd make it a home—a house where Jesus' love would surround and sustain us.

Poverty was not found in heaven. It abounded on earth, but man did not know its value. The Son of God, therefore, treasured it and came down from heaven to choose it for himself, to make it precious to us.

— St. Bernard of Clairvaux

SHINE YOUR LIGHT

> You are the light of the world. A city set on a mountain cannot be hidden. Nor do they light a lamp and then put it under a bushel basket; it is set on a lampstand, where it gives light to all in the house. Just so, your light must shine before others, that they may see your good deeds and glorify your heavenly Father.
>
> — Mt 5:14-16

It didn't take us long to pack our things, because we had been flown to Kentucky with just suitcases, and our two children. Our friends at Earthwood Farm could not understand what we were doing, and we gave up trying to explain. We felt so excited and so free as we drove away, and up the driveway of our new little home. We had known it was right, and that it was God's gift to us, but the reality started to hit as we began to settle in. What was that smell? We had already cleaned up the dead opossum—what on earth was it? Then we saw, only a few feet from the house, a pig barn—crammed full of about 100 pigs being fattened up! We wondered why we hadn't noticed it. Perhaps God had closed our eyes (and our noses) to it before!

Oh well, that's country life! We stood outside looking at the beautiful pastoral scene. The Appaloosa horses grazed nearby; we were surrounded by meadows and rolling hills. The realization came to us then... that we had nothing but the clothes on our backs, and the few in the suitcases we'd brought. How were we going to live? We'd been working as volunteers at Earthwood Farm, and had all our needs covered there. What were we doing? How irresponsible we felt; how could we be so foolish as to throw away the opportunity of a lifetime for THIS?! We began to express these doubts to each other. But we had felt so right about it—it had to be right! Didn't it?

6 **Proclaiming Christ means above all giving witness to him with one's life. It is the simplest**

> form of preaching the Gospel and, at the same
> time, the most effective way available to you. It
> consists in showing he visible presence of
> Christ in one's own life by a daily commitment
> and by making every concrete decision in con-
> formity with the Gospel.
>
> — Pope John Paul II

As these misgivings were nagging at us,
and anxiety about the future, we noticed a
couple of old pick-up trucks coming up the
driveway. They looked familiar, and as they
got closer, we noticed that it was the Families
of St Benedict! They were smiling and wav-
ing, and as they got out, they started to
empty their trucks. They brought in bedding,
towels, dishes, pots, and large quantities of
bulk food in jars. They even brought toys for
the children, and little handmade gifts for us.
We were overwhelmed—suddenly we had
everything we needed, and from people who
barely had enough to get by themselves. We
knew that they were giving from their *need*,
rather than from their surplus. We felt so
inadequate to express our gratitude, and

when we tried, they just told us simply: "It's just the love of Jesus!"

We noticed two figures coming over the hill from the monastery. It was Brother Frederic and Brother Maurice, bringing homemade ice cream and guitars for a house-warming welcome party! The joy and singing and dancing would resound in our ears for many years to come, reminding us how much God loves us through his people!

Love is a fire. It must spend itself in service. Service is the dry wood for the fire of love that makes it burst into a bonfire that reaches into eternity and burns there. We must be a flame in the darkness, a lamp to our neighbour's feet, a place where he can warm himself, a place where he can see the face of God.

— Catherine Doherty

GOD'S INCREDIBLE MERCY

Our sins that are past, why even remember
them? God has forgotten them. Why is it
that we want to remember them? A forgiv-
en sin does not exist in the mind of God.
God is not a stingy forgiver who remem-
bers our sins for the rest of our life. The
mercy of God is infinite!

— Catherine Doherty

While we were living in the beautiful
broken-down house, Don was asked
one day if he could help plant some oak trees
on the monastery farm. He was honoured to
be included in the life of the cloistered
monastery, with monks who had a vow of
silence and chanted prayers seven times a
day. Brother René, a quiet gentle man by
nature anyway, worked beside Don, as they
planted the little oak seedlings. It was quiet,
meditative work, but Brother René spoke to
Don now and then, and Don felt honoured to
hear his soft and wise words.

Don picked up a seedling that was broken and twisted, and asked: "What do you think, Brother Rene, should I just chuck it out?"

Brother René stopped what he was doing and looked over at the little broken seedling in Don's hands. He looked up, and smiled at Don and said softly: "Oh no, plant it—we give them all a chance…"

The words penetrated and resonated deep within Don, and he tenderly placed the little broken seedling in the ground, and he thanked God that *he too* had been given a chance. Not because he deserved it, but just because God loved him so much.

> Listening to the Word in an attitude of prayer, contemplation, wonder and certainty, say to God : "I need you, I count on you in order to exist and to live. You are stronger than my sin. I believe in your power over my life, I believe that you are able to save me just as I am now. Remember me. Pardon me!"
>
> — Pope John Paul II

Our Mother Mary

In our age, so many young people are desperately seeking a mother, for so many mothers are not there for their children. Mary is there, for she is the mother of humanity. She is the one who will console and understand and take youth by the hand and lead them to her Son, whom they are seeking so constantly, so endlessly.

— Catherine Doherty

Don walked to the early morning mass through the dew-covered fields of the monastery. He was grappling with something deep within. Sure, the Virgin Mary was real, but what was the big deal about her? Did he have to worship her? He'd been brought up to believe that praying to her was a sin, and could even lead him to hell.

He passed close to one of the little hermitages along the way, and noticed someone coming out. He recognized Brother René,

whom he had just met yesterday while help-
ing the monks to plant trees. Although he
would have loved to engage in conversation
with him, and drink his words of wisdom
once more, he realized that his time planting
trees with him had been a privileged occa-
sion. Now he was back to his vow of silence.
It made Don see how important words are,
and how careful we should all be in choosing
what comes out of our mouths. He waved at
Brother Rene, and continued to walk on
towards the chapel, but he noticed the monk
beckoning to him. As he drew near, he saw
that he was holding something in his hands,
and as he reached him, he placed some beads
in Don's hands. Don liked to wear beads, but
was surprised that Brother Rene would give
him such a gift.

"These are two rosaries for you and Posie.
They are prayer beads, and they are made
from seeds of a flower called Job's tears. I
stayed up last night and made them for you,
and had them blessed by the abbot at Lauds."
He handed him two little pamphlets. "Here
are the instructions for praying—each bead

represents a prayer. Mary is your mother, and as you pray with her she will reveal herself to you more and more, and lead you to her son Jesus. She will always walk beside you and help you to be a Christian."

If you follow Mary you will not swerve from the right path; if you pray to her you will not fall into despair; if she holds you, you will not fall; if she protects you, you need not fear; if she leads you, you will never weary; and if she befriends you, you will be safe.

— St. Bernard

Don looked down at the beautiful silvery seeds that were beads, and the crucifix. He knew that this was a turning point, and that he would pray with these beads and get to know his Mother Mary. His doubts about her were already beginning to dissolve. He knew that through this prayer, he would be able to allow her to love him and lead him.

Young people who are listening to me: in times when doubts, difficulties and sadness confront you, know that the Virgin Mary is your consolation and peace; Mary asks you for your 'yes'. She asks you to make a radical commitment to Christ. She asks you to dare to follow him by placing your lives in God's hands, so that he might make of you instruments for a better world than the one in which we live. Mary is hoping that you will generously answer the call of her Son if he asks you to give everything.

— Pope John Paul II

Coming Home

The one who began a good work in you will continue to complete it until the day of Christ Jesus.

— Phil 1:6

Over the course of several months, we journeyed through the Apostles' Creed with Brother Frederic, and felt we were beginning to understand more about God and His Church. Although we had come so far, and learned so much, we knew that our time here was nearly up, and we pondered where we should go from there. Our whole life had changed completely, and we needed to settle down with our family, which was soon to be blessed with a new child. In discussing the situation with Brother Frederic, he had a couple of suggestions.

"Since you seem attracted to community life, I've heard of a wonderful community up in Michigan that has a very lively faith—they are referred to as Charismatics, and many of them are Catholic. I think you might really fit in, and could enter the Church there. But you'd still have the visa problem." He stopped momentarily, and then continued:

"But I have another idea. A priest from a Catholic community in Canada gave a retreat to the monks recently, and touched a lot of hearts. They are in a tiny little village in Ontario called Combermere, I think. The community is called Madonna House. I could give you his name if you'd like. They live a simple rural lifestyle—I think it might suit you really well."

Don and I looked at one another and laughed. We were learning that there were no coincidences in God. We had lived twenty miles from there a few years before, with a number of other back-to-the-landers. We had known Madonna House because of their used clothing centre and library, and remembered the warmth and openness of those we had met there. God seemed to be pointing us back there, this time with new faith and new perspective. Perhaps they could water the seed that had been planted in our hearts, and bring us into the Catholic Church.

> It is only by following that strange voice that says 'Come on, higher' that my faith and your faith will grow. It is the growth in faith that will make us understand the immense hunger of our heart. And, strangely enough, the hunger of our heart is a desire for obedience to that voice.
>
> — Catherine Doherty

We returned to our cabin in Northern Ontario first, where we gave birth to our third daughter. Having left our decorated bus in Canada, we were happy to reclaim it and soon were on the road again, heading for Combermere. Our "Sunship" now became the "Sonship" as we turned our lives over to the Son of God.

Pulling into the parking lot at Madonna House, Don got out to scout around for someone who could lead us to Father Pelton, our contact from Brother Frederic. He met a woman sitting on the doorstep who was friendly and welcoming. He asked her if she worked there, and she told him that she did. He seemed to get the idea that she was the cleaning lady. When he told her I was out in our bus with the children, she asked if she could climb in to meet the family. She told us that her name was 'B'. Even if she had mentioned that her real name was Catherine de Hueck Doherty, it would have meant nothing to us. It was only later we learned that she was the foundress of Madonna House, and the author of a best-selling book, called *Poustinia*. She simply accepted us and loved us as we were, and showed deep interest in our life and our children. She told us wonderful stories about delivering babies in the surrounding area, before the hospital was built.

Hers was the unconditional love we were to experience from all the staff we were to meet there, and it was their love that continued the work begun by God in Kentucky—drawing us into Jesus' heart, and into His Church.

Love... love... love, never counting the cost.

— Catherine Doherty

TAKING THE LEAP

Trust in the LORD with all your heart,
    on your own intelligence rely not;
In all your ways be mindful of him,
    and he will make straight your paths.

— Prov 3:5-6

Two years had now gone by since our walks with Brother Frederic in the Kentucky hills. In that time we had met other Christians in the Combermere area, and had formed an interfaith prayer group with a few other families. We met weekly in each other's homes to pray and support one another in living our Christian Faith. We visited other Christian churches, and were welcomed warmly in each one, sometimes being invited to sing our Kentucky-influenced gospel music. One Sunday we played at the Catholic Church and the Pentecostal Church in the same day, travelling between the two in our colourful bus, with our three children in tow.

Much as we enjoyed these friendships and experienced God's presence in these other churches we attended, there was a hunger in us which wasn't being satisfied. In the back of our mind we knew that it was Jesus in the Eucharist who was calling us into the Catholic Church. He was calling us to let go of our doubts, our prejudices, but most of all our pride, and submit to him through his Church.

Let us love the Church with a passionate love. Let us remember that the Church, in its sacraments and in its very being, is a mystery of love, because Christ, its head, is a mystery of love. Let us first incarnate this mystery of love in our lives, and only afterward turn our eyes to the human vessels of clay. But let us do this latter reverently, with hearts full of charity, patience and understanding. Otherwise the fog of confusion and of chaos will take hold of us and we shall be out of touch with God who is Love.

— Catherine Doherty

The pristine purity of the monks chanting and the masses at the monastery were a hard act to follow. We were drawn to the liturgy and the faith at Madonna House, but they reminded us gently that ordinary parish life was the way of holiness for us. We were called to enter into a parish, and receive the sacraments along with everyone else. Although the Church is the Bride of Christ, it is made up out of weak humans, just like us.

Just like us...Something suddenly broke in us. We were like everyone else...we were no better and no worse than the rest of God's people...we were just different parts of this colourful patchwork. We didn't have to fight the system anymore: just our own tendency to sin. The stubborn pride of youth gave way to a surge of love for all our brothers and sisters in Christ. The fear of 'giving in' to a two-thousand-year-old institution seemed to just melt away. Our hearts were softened and open, and we were hungry for God. We wanted to learn and grow and serve God's Church in whatever way we could. We were

ready to trustingly jump off the cliff into our
Father's arms.

Be patient with the Church! The Church is
always a community of weak and imperfect
individuals. And I would like to add: this is at
the same time all for the best. For there would
indeed be no room for us in a Church of perfect men...He wants us human beings to be his
collaborators in the world and in the Church,
with all our deficiencies and short-comings, but
with all our good will and capabilities as well.
He wants you too!
— Pope John Paul II

We stood inside the simple little A-frame
chapel and made our profession of faith. The
scent of pine trees wafted through the screen
door, and the birds singing outside seemed to
echo our love song—our 'yes' to God and his
Church. The chapel was at Madonna House's
family camp, Cana Colony, where we had just
spent a week with our family. God had been
good to us; we had made new friends, and
our homespun catechesis had been complet-
ed.

As I repeated those now familiar words from the creed that drew me into the Church, I knew that I was saying 100% yes to God and his Church—and all its teachings. I couldn't do it in a half-hearted manner. I knew that no matter what would come our way, the Church would teach and guide us in ways that were the very best for us. Here was contained the truth that would set us free. We surrendered our wills to God, and received the true freedom we had been searching for our whole lives.

Nothing was ever the same after that day. It was a brand new beginning, but in a very true sense, a coming home to stay.

Nothing half-hearted for me—I will follow Christ with all my heart and soul.

— St. Therese of Lisieux

LITTLE MANDATE BOOKS

This set of handsome keepsake books collects the wisdom of the Church's greatest teachers and saints on the holiest of vocations—marriage and parenthood.

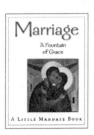

The timeless wisdom of the Holy Father, Pope John Paul II, and Catherine Doherty, foundress of Madonna House, is featured prominently in this new series of books. The theme of Catherine's *Little Mandate*—a beautiful distillation of the Gospel of Jesus—weaves throughout and serves as an important foundation. Each book also gives an abundance of brief and profound quotations from Holy Scripture, and quotations from some of the great Catholic saints.

These books are small enough to carry anywhere—and their wisdom is arranged in bite-size segments that you can read on the run, whenever you can spare time.

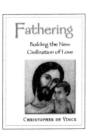

Marriage: A Fountain of Grace

Mothering: Becoming the Heart of the Home

Fathering: Building the New Civilization of Love

Each book: $6.95 U.S. — $8.95 Canadian

Order Toll Free: 1-888-703-7110

MADONNA HOUSE PUBLICATIONS

COMBERMERE • ONTARIO • CANADA • K0J 1L0

"Lord, give bread to the hungry, and hunger for you to those who have bread," was a favourite prayer of our foundress, Catherine Doherty. At Madonna House Publications, we strive to satisfy the spiritual hunger for God in our modern world with the timeless words of the Gospel message.

Faithful to the teachings of the Catholic Church and its magisterium, Madonna House Publications is a non-profit apostolate dedicated to publishing high quality and easily accessible books, audiobooks, videos and music. We pray our publications will awaken and deepen in our readers an experience of Jesus' love in the most simple and ordinary facets of everyday life.

Your generosity can help Madonna House Publications provide the poor around the world with editions of important spiritual works containing the enduring wisdom of the Gospel message. If you would like to help, please send your contribution to the address below. We also welcome your questions and comments. May God bless you for your participation in this apostolate.

Madonna House Publications
2888 Dafoe Rd
Combermere ON K0J 1L0
Canada

Internet: www.madonnahouse.org/publications